What Happens When We Recycle

Glass?

Jillian Powell

W

FRANKLIN WATTS

LONDON • SYDNEY

This edition © 2014 Franklin Watts
338 Euston Road, London NW1 3BH

Franklin Watts Australia
Level 17/207 Kent Street
Sydney NSW 2000

Editor: Julia Bird
Designer: DR Ink
Art Director: Jonathan Hair

Picture credits: Andrew Brookes/Corbis: 15b; Paul
Bricknell: 26; Chris Fairclough: 11t; Graham Flack/Waste
Watch: 16, 17t; Christine Glade/istockphoto: 6t; Chris
Howes/Wild Places/Alamy: 8; Image 100/Corbis: 6b;
Keystone/Topfoto: 12; Will & Deni McIntyre/Corbis: 10;
Moodboard/Corbis: 11b; Hank Morgan/SPL: 20, 21.
NASA: 9br; Vladimir Popovic/Shutterstock: 25b;
Proteus/Waste Watch: 24b; Ray Roberts/Alamy: 14.
Helene Rogers/Alamy: 25t; Rockware Glass Ltd: 18, 19
Steve Sant/Alamy: 22; Jerome Scholler/Shuttrestock: 23br;
Volker Steger/SPL: 7; Jan Suttle/Alamy; 15t; Franz-Peter
Tschauner/epa/Corbis: 13, 23t; Jim Winkley/Ecoscene: 9c;
Wrap/Waste Watch: 24t.

Every attempt has been made to clear copyright. Should
there be any inadvertent omission please apply to the
Publishers for rectification.

A CIP catalogue record for this book
is available from the British Library

ISBN: 978 1 4451 3028 6

Dewey Classification: 363.72'88

Printed in China

Franklin Watts is a division of
Hachette Children's Books,
an Hachette UK company.
www.hachette.co.uk

Contents

About glass

What is glass?

Glass is an important **material** because it is strong and **transparent**. People have been using glass for around 5,000 years.

Baby food is often sold in glass jars.

Glass is easy to wipe clean.

Uses

Today, we use glass to make all sorts of things, from windows and doors to TV and computer screens, light bulbs and kitchenware. Glass bottles and jars are strong, **hygienic** containers for food and drinks, medicines and household products.

New glass

The UK glass industry makes around six billion new bottles and jars each year. The average UK family uses around 330 glass bottles or jars at home in a year.

How it's made

Glass is made by melting together **raw materials**, including sand, **soda ash** and **limestone**, until the mixture is **molten** or liquid. When it is molten, glass can be made into many different shapes. As it cools, it hardens again.

Glass is made in a **furnace** at very high temperatures.

Why recycle glass?

● Buried rubbish

Every year, we use around 3.6 million tonnes of glass in the UK. About 1.2 million tonnes is recycled; the rest is thrown away in **landfill sites**. Unlike many materials, glass does not **decompose**. Instead, it stays buried in the ground forever.

JUST THE FACTS

Glass makes up about 8% of household rubbish by weight and 2% by **volume**.

Glass and other rubbish is filling up more and more of our landfill sites.

The environment

Recycling glass reduces the amount of glass put into landfill. Recycling also saves the **energy** and raw materials needed to make new glass. This helps the environment in two main ways. It reduces the **quarrying** of raw materials. It also decreases the amount of **carbon emissions** produced by burning fuel in glass furnaces.

Limestone quarrying harms the environment.

? DID YOU KNOW?

The amount of glass recycled every year saves enough energy to launch ten space shuttles!

Collection

● Kerbside collection

Some glass is collected from households in recycling boxes. Vans collect the boxes and sort different types of waste, such as glass, paper and cans, into piles.

● Bottle banks

You can also take glass to bottle banks. Most banks sort bottles into clear, brown and green glass.

Everyone can take part in recycling.

GREEN GUIDE

Before recycling glass, remove any bottle tops or jar lids and rinse the container in water to remove any leftover food or drink.

Lorries

Special recycling lorries collect the glass from bottle banks. They are divided into three sections to keep clear, brown and green glass separate.

Recycling workers sort the glass into the right sections.

JUST THE FACTS

- The UK has over 50,000 bottle banks.
- Each bank can hold up to 3,000 bottles.
- About one in five households has a kerbside collection.

GREEN GUIDE

Glass products that can and can't be recycled:

✓ bottles and jars

✗ light bulbs, drinking glasses, mirrors, computer or TV screens

Most recycling boxes are collected once a week.

recycle

Sorting

A load of green glass is delivered to the plant, ready to be recycled.

At the plant

Lorries transport glass from bottle banks to the recycling plant. First, they tip it into large loading bays. Then a shovel moves the glass into one of three giant **hoppers** on the side of the recycling plant. Each hopper takes clear, green or brown glass.

Conveyor belt

The hopper drops the glass onto a moving **conveyor belt**. This belt carries the glass into the recycling plant.

?

DID YOU KNOW?

Coloured glass protects food or drink contents from light. Once colour is added to glass, it cannot be removed. Half of all the glass we recycle is green.

Waste check

The glass has to be very thoroughly cleaned at different stages of the recycling process. First, the conveyor belt passes through a picking station. Here, workers check the glass and pick out any big bits of waste, such as bottle tops, corks or lids.

Workers wear thick gloves to protect their hands from the broken glass.

Colour sorting

Colour coding

If glass has been collected from homes or mixed recycling bins, it needs to be sorted by colour when it arrives at the recycling plant. Some plants have special colour-sorting units. At other plants, workers sort the glass by hand.

JUST THE FACTS

Colour-sorting units can sort around ten tonnes of glass an hour.

Some glass recycling plants receive as much as 600 tonnes of glass a day.

Colour sorting units can be set to remove one or more colours of glass.

Light rays

The colour sorting unit pushes the glass over a plate that has **fibre optic cables** in it. When light rays are sent through the glass, the cables detect colours by how much light passes through each piece of glass. Powerful air jets then fire away any pieces that are the wrong colour.

?

DID YOU KNOW?

Coloured glass is made by adding different metal or mineral salts to it. Brown and green glass, for example, are made by adding iron to the glass while it is being melted.

Crushing

● Cullet

The conveyor belt carries the glass to a machine that has large metal rollers.

The rollers crush the glass into little bits as it passes between them. The crushed glass is called **cullet**.

This glass is being crushed to make cullet. A piece of cullet measures between 10 and 55mm.

16

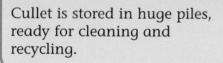

Cullet is stored in huge piles, ready for cleaning and recycling.

GREEN GUIDE

Make sure that none of these waste materials gets in with your glass for recycling:

- stones and dirt
- metal tops and lids
- lead and wire rings
- **ceramic** cups and plates
- plastic CD sleeves
- drinking glasses
- food or drink contents.

Items like these should not be included with your glass for recycling.

Cleaning

● Using magnets

Next, the cullet passes under a strong **magnet**. The magnet pulls out any pieces of **ferrous** metal or wire from lids, bottle tops or ring-pulls.

DID YOU KNOW?

Magnets attract ferrous metals. A magnet has an invisible force called a **magnetic field**. It pulls metals like iron and steel towards it.

Strong magnets take out pieces of metal from the cullet.

● Other metals

The cullet then passes over a metal separator, which takes out any bits of non-ferrous metals like lead or aluminium. Jets of air blow them away down into a waste chute.

Screening

The cleaned cullet then goes over two **vibrating** screens One shakes out small pieces of waste material, such as wire or paper, that were missed at the picking station. The other removes any chips of stone and ceramics left in the glass.

Laser beams pick out any stray materials left in the cullet.

Vacuum

The cullet then passes under a vacuum that sucks up any bits of paper from labels or plastic packaging.

Laser or x-rays

Finally, a machine shines **laser beams** or **x-rays** onto the cullet. These pass through glass but they are reflected off any other materials. These are blown down a waste chute, leaving just the pure, clean cullet.

Checking and sampling

Samples

Workers at the recycling plant take samples of cullet to check its quality. They put the samples into a machine that tests how pure the cullet is. If there are any bits of waste still mixed in with the cullet, the machine weighs and records them on a computer.

A worker holds a handful of green cullet, which is ready for sampling.

Quality checks

The machine works out how pure one tonne of the sampled cullet is. If it is not pure enough, the cullet will have to go through the cleaning processes again before it can be sent on to glass factories.

A quality controller carries out the final checks on a batch of cullet before it goes to be recycled.

JUST THE FACTS

A tonne of cullet must contain less than 20 grams of waste matter before it is used to make recycled glass. This is about the same as one tablespoon of sugar in a thousand bags of sugar!

Moulding

Gobs

The clean cullet is taken to a glass factory to be made into new bottles and jars. The cullet is mixed with limestone, sand and soda ash, and then goes into a furnace. The heat melts the glass and a machine cuts it into **gobs**.

? DID YOU KNOW?

Cullet can make up over 90% of a recycled glass object.

Glass gobs can be made by machines or by glassblowers, using a tool called a blow pipe.

Moulding

The glass gobs pass into a machine where they are pressed and blown into **moulds** to form bottles and jars.

80% of recycled glass is made into bottles and jars.

Samples

As the new containers are made, samples are taken to check the quality of the glass. The bottles and jars are then ready to be sent to food and drink manufacturers to be filled.

GREEN GUIDE

Look out for the 'loop' symbol that tells you a bottle or jar can be recycled. It may also mean the container is made from recycled glass.

New products

● Building

As well as making new bottles and jars, recycled glass can be used for building. Crushed glass can be mixed with other materials to make road surfaces, clay for house bricks, and as decoration.

Some glass can be made into fibreglass **insulation** for roofs. Insulation keeps houses warm and saves energy used for heating.

These tiles are made of ConGlassCrete, a mixture of concrete and recycled glass.

JUST THE FACTS

Around 150,000 tonnes of recycled glass is used for road building each year, helping to reduce quarrying of rock, sand and gravel.

Recycled glass can be mixed with other materials for use in building.

A vase made from recycled glass.

● Cleaning

Recycled glass can be used to clean graffiti off buildings or to make metal smooth for painting.

Glass can be also used instead of sand to filter and clean water for swimming pools, fish farms or drinking water systems.

What you can do

CASE STUDY

Schools in Wales have been working in partnership with the Recycled Bottle Glass Centre in Newport. Each school commissions a stained glass panel and pupils are invited to work on ideas and designs. The Glass Centre holds a workshop at the school showing children how they make the panel from recycled glass. The finished panel then goes on display in the school.

5 top tips for glass recyclers:

1
Buy products in glass rather than plastic – it's easier to recycle!

2
Remove tops and rinse out bottles and jars before recycling.

3
Only recycle glass bottles or jars. Milk bottles must go back to the milkman - they can be used up to 20 times.

4
Remember to sort colours – blue glass goes in the green bin.

5
Try not to put glass into the bottle bank at night-time when it will disturb others.

Hanging jar lanterns

You will need:

Three jam jars with rims
Garden wire
Glass or acrylic paint and brush

Wire cutters
Pliers
Three tea lights

Step 1
Paint the outside of each jar with different coloured patterns and allow to dry.

Step 2
Measure enough wire to loop around the rim of the jar and to make a handle. Leave about 4cm extra and ask an adult to cut it with the wire cutters.

Step 3
Form the wire into an S shape and use the pliers to pinch small loops either end.

Step 4
Attach one loop to make a ring to go around the rim of the jar.

Step 5
Fit the ring over the jar, then attach the other loop to form the handle. Use the pliers to tighten the loops.

Step 5
Pour a little sea salt or sand inside each jam jar and place the tea light on top. Ask an adult to help you light your lantern.

Glossary

Carbon emissions   Gases that are believed to cause climate change. Climate change is a gradual change in the world's weather.

Ceramic   A shiny material made from fired clay.

Conveyor belt   A moving belt which transports things, for example through a recycling plant or factory.

Cullet   Tiny pieces of crushed glass.

Decompose   Break down.

Energy   Power or heat.

Ferrous   Containing the metal iron.

Fibre optic cables   Cables made from glass or plastic that can carry light.

Flat glass   Glass that is used to make TV and computer screens and windows, among many other things.

Furnace   A huge burner used in industry.

Fuse   To join by heating and melting.

Gobs   Lumps or pieces.

Hoppers   Large containers.

Hygienic   Very clean.

Insulation   Material that keeps warmth in.

Kiln   A very hot oven used for firing pottery, glass or bricks.

Landfill sites   Places where rubbish is buried under the ground.

Laser beams   A kind of light ray.

Limestone   A kind of chalky rock.

Magnet   A piece of metal that can draw ferrous substances towards it.

Magnetic field   An invisible field surrounding a magnet that draws substances containing iron towards it.

Material   A substance that something else is made from.

Mineral   A substance that is found in nature.

Molten   When something solid melts and becomes liquid.

Moulds   Containers that shape materials as the materials harden.

Quarrying   Digging out of the ground.

Raw materials Natural materials, such as wood and water.

Soda ash   Sodium carbonate in powder form.

Transparent   See-through.

Vibrating   Slightly shaking

Volume   The amount of space that something takes up.

X-rays   Electro-magnetic rays that can pass through solid materials.

Further information

Books

Environment Detective Investigates: Reducing & Recycling Waste Jen Green, Wayland 2010

Glass (Recycling and Reusing Materials) Ruth Thomson and Neil Thomson, Franklin Watts 2006

How It's Made: A Glass Jar Sarah Ridley, Franklin Watts 2006

Websites

www.glassforever.co.uk
An interactive website with games, facts and advice on recycling glass.

www.glassrecycle.co.uk
The website for one of Britain's largest glass recycling companies, with lots of useful facts and figures.

www.recyclingglass.co.uk
A fun interactive website about recycling glass.

Index